CENGAGE Learning·

Novels for Students, Volume 35

Project Editor: Sara Constantakis Rights Acquisition and Management: Margaret Chamberlain-Gaston, Leitha Etheridge-Sims, Kelly Quin, Aja Perales Composition: Evi Abou-El-Seoud Manufacturing: Drew Kalasky

Imaging: John Watkins

Product Design: Pamela A. E. Galbreath, Jennifer Wahi Content Conversion: Katrina Coach Product Manager: Meggin Condino © 2011 Gale, Cengage

For product information and technology assistance, contact us at **Gale Customer Support, 1-800-877-4253.**

For permission to use material from this text or product, submit all requests online at **www.cengage.com/permissions**.

Further permissions questions can be emailed to **permissionrequest@cengage.com** While every effort has been made to ensure the reliability of the information presented in this publication, Gale, a part of Cengage Learning, does not guarantee the accuracy of the data contained herein. Gale accepts no payment for listing; and inclusion in the publication of any organization, agency, institution, publication, service, or individual does not imply endorsement of the editors or publisher. Errors brought to the attention of the publisher and verified to the satisfaction of the publisher will be corrected in future editions.

Gale
27500 Drake Rd.
Farmington Hills, MI, 48331-3535

ISBN-13: 978-1-4144-6698-9
ISBN-10: 1-4144-6698-6
ISSN 1094-3552

This title is also available as an e-book.
ISBN-13: 978-1-4144-7364-2

ISBN-10: 1-4144-7364-8
Contact your Gale, a part of Cengage Learning sales
representative for ordering information.

Printed in the United States of America
1 2 3 4 5 6 7 14 13 12 11 10

Oroonoko; or, The Royal Slave: A True History

Aphra Behn

1688

Introduction

Aphra Behn is credited with being the first female professional writer in England. In 1688, as a well-established dramatist, Behn published *Oroonoko; or, The Royal Slave: A True History* (also known by the shorter title *Oroonoko*), the story of an African prince who is forced into slavery in the South American country of Suriname, which in the late 1600s was an English colony. In her dedication to the work, Behn claims the story is true and establishes herself as the narrator in the novel. Scholars conjecture that Behn likely visited the English colony in the 1660s and based her work on her experiences there. The veracity of Behn's account is an area of modern critical debate.

In Behn's novel, the warrior prince, Oroonoko, falls in love with a young maiden, Imoinda, whom the king of their nation takes as his mistress. When the young lovers are discovered together, Imoinda is sold into slavery. Duped by an English slave trader with whom he has previously done business, Oroonoko is also captured and sold. Although he is purchased as a slave, Oroonoko impresses the plantation's overseer and is allowed to live separately from the other slaves and to do no work. After Oroonoko discovers Imoinda has been sold to the same plantation, the lovers conceive a child and attempt to bargain with their captors to return to Africa. Realizing that they will not be allowed to leave, Oroonoko leads a mass escape from the plantation. The group is quickly overtaken by the English, and Oroonoko is punished. Fearing Imoinda will be tortured, Oroonoko kills her, and he is subsequently tortured and executed. Throughout the tale, the narrator stresses Oroonoko's nobility and expresses her deep sympathy for him. At the time the work was published, *Oroonoko* was treated as a romance, the love between Oroonoko and Imoinda being viewed as the work's main theme. Later critics have focused on the novel as an exploration of imperialism, slavery, and true nobility.

Originally published in 1688 by William Canning, along with two other works, in the volume *Three Histories: Oroonoko, The Fair Jilt, Agnes de Castro, Oroonoko* is available in a 2003 Penguin Classics edition.

Author Biography

Little is actually known about Behn's life, particularly her youth. It is believed that she was born around 1640, in Canterbury, in the county of Kent, in England, to parents thought to be named Bartholomew and Elizabeth Johnson. Scholars speculate that around 1663, perhaps earlier, Behn visited the English colony established by Lord Willoughby in Suriname (now the Republic of Suriname). Although it has been theorized that Behn's father was a lieutenant-general in Suriname, based on the narrator's account in *Oroonoko*, most scholars believe Behn's parents to be of humbler birth. Once she returned to London, Behn likely married a German merchant, Johan Behn. The mysterious husband disappeared from her life shortly after; either he died, or the couple separated. In 1666, Behn was sent by the English government as a royalist agent to Antwerp, Belgium, to work as a spy. With England at war with the Dutch, Behn was assigned to gather information from a William Scot, who was providing information on the Dutch to England through Behn. Allegedly duped by Scot, Behn was cut from the English payroll and returned to London in great poverty.

At this point, Behn began to write plays for the English stage. Her first, *The Forc'd Marriage*, premiered in 1670. After the success of this play, Behn penned a number of subsequent plays. Some of her dramas were political in nature and supportive of the government of King Charles II. Behn also successfully published as a poet, and her work was known for its erotic nature, and she for her promiscuity. In 1688, following the success of her plays and poetry, Behn published *Three Histories: Oroonoko, The Fair Jilt, Agnes de Castro*. Two of these stories (*Oroonoko* and *The Fair Jilt*) are based on Behn's experiences in Suriname. In the last years of her life, Behn witnessed two royal transitions. After Charles's death and James II's ascension to the throne in 1685, James was ousted only a few years later. Just before Behn's death in 1689, James's daughter Mary and her husband William were crowned queen and king.

The Epistle Dedicatory

Oroonoko, whose full title is *Oroonoko; or, The Royal Slave: A True History*, is prefaced by a letter of dedication, or "epistle dedicatory." In this dedication, Behn addresses the Lord Maitland, a Scottish minister under King James II, whose literary activities Behn admired. After praising Maitland's "wit and worth," Behn spends the better part of a long paragraph explaining why a man with known faults may still be praised for his virtues, and she argues that such a man's true nobility reveals itself through his written works. Behn goes on to applaud Maitland's scholarly nature, his quest for knowledge, and his writings in which he defends the Catholic Church and explicates its teachings. Maitland's personal life and marriage are also the subject of Behn's effusive compliments. Behn then turns to her story, explaining to Maitland that what he is about to read is a true story. She defends the work against being labeled romantic (depicting an idealized world in the paradisiacal country of Suriname) by pointing out that the country she describes is extremely different from England and is full of wondrous things that may be hard to imagine, although Behn has truthfully written about them. Asking Maitland to forgive any faults in the book, Behn explains that she wrote it in a few hours.

Media Adaptations

- *Oroonoko* is available on audio CD, published by Babblebooks in 2008.

The History of the Royal Slave

As Behn opens her story, she explains that while she was an eyewitness to what the royal slave endured after he came to Suriname, the earlier part of his story, which concerns Oroonoko's youth and how he came to be captured, is based on what Oroonoko told her. Behn narrates the story in the first person, referring to herself as "I." In the dedication and in the opening paragraphs, she identifies herself as the story's narrator. For the next several pages, Behn describes the native inhabitants of Suriname, the "Indians," as she states. At length she catalogues the various items the Indians trade with English colonists, which the English in turn take back to England to sell. Behn discusses some of the life and daily habits of the Indians. The English colonists lived "in perfect tranquility and good understanding" with these native people, for, as Behn points out, it benefited the colonists to do so, as the Indians knew the land and where to hunt. The Indians also greatly outnumbered the colonists, Behn observes, so the English did not dare attempt to use them as slaves.

This statement allows Behn the opportunity to transition from a discussion of Suriname to the place where her story actually begins, in Africa, the country where the English acquired the slaves to work the Suriname sugar plantations. In the African nation of Coramantien, slaves are bought by the English and brought back to Suriname. (As Janet Todd explains in the footnotes to the 2003 Penguin edition of *Oroonoko*, Coramantien, or Koromantyn, was a trading post on Africa's west coast, an area that corresponds roughly with the coast of modern Ghana.)

Describing the structure of this nation, Behn characterizes it as a warrior society, ruled by an ancient king. On the battlefield, the young royal, Prince Oroonoko, who is the grandson of the old king, has earned a reputation as brave and daring. At the age of seventeen he becomes a general, when his commander is killed in battle. Behn paints a picture of the prince in which he is depicted as physically perfect and beautiful. Her description emphasizes the way his features are more European than African. Oroonoko falls in love with the daughter of his fallen commander, a girl named Imoinda, and to honor her he presents her with the slaves who have been captured in a recent battle. Imoinda returns Oroonoko's affections. The young couple make vows to one another.

The old king has, like Oroonoko, noticed Imoinda's exceptional beauty. Despite the fact that he has learned that Oroonoko and Imoinda are romantically involved, the king, who already has many wives and mistresses, desires her for himself. He sends Imoinda his royal veil, a symbol that designates Imoinda as the king's possession, his mistress. In keeping with the culture of their society, Imoinda cannot refuse the king's command. When Oroonoko learns that Imoinda has become the king's mistress, he is devastated. He knows that to rebel against the king would result in death for both himself and his beloved Imoinda.

With the help of a fellow warrior, Aboan, and one of the king's discarded mistresses, Onahal, who now tends to Imoinda, Oroonoko manages to spend a few stolen hours with Imoinda. When the king discovers that Oroonoko and Imoinda have been together, he sells Imoinda as a slave and has Oroonoko told that Imoinda has been executed. Gradually, the king begins to feel remorse for having wronged Oroonoko. Fearing that Oroonoko will plot revenge against him, he seeks Oroonoko's pardon. Oroonoko carries on, but he grieves for Imoinda.

When an English slave trader, with whom

Oroonoko has previously conducted business, arrives, he invites Oroonoko and his companions aboard his ship, apparently as guests. Soon, however, Oroonoko and the others are overcome and bound, and they are destined to be sold as slaves. They are taken to Suriname, and Oroonoko is sold to a plantation owner. The overseer, named Trefry, who purchases Oroonoko is impressed by Oroonoko's regal bearing, his fine attire, his intelligence, and his ability to speak English. Trefry allows Oroonoko to live apart from the other slaves and to not work. Trefry promises that the situation is temporary and that he will endeavor to return Oroonoko to his own country. As is the custom with all the African slaves at the Suriname plantation to which Oroonoko has been taken, Oroonoko is renamed. Trefry calls him Caesar. When Oroonoko meets the other slaves at the plantation, he finds that they are people who he himself sold to the English. Knowing Oroonoko's royal status, they revere him and remain loyal to him.

Trefry tells Oroonoko about a female slave who has recently been brought to the plantation, a girl whom all the male slaves desire. The girl has been named Clemene, but when Oroonoko meets her he finds that she is none other than Imoinda. The lovers, who made their vows to one another in Africa, are allowed to live together as husband and wife, and they conceive a child. With Imoinda pregnant, Oroonoko continues to seek freedom for himself and his wife. He offers wealth and slaves in return for their passage home. As Behn points out, the slaveholders have no intention of letting

Oroonoko go, but they pacify him by allowing him to hunt and to have more freedom than any of the other slaves at the plantation. Oroonoko even serves as an intermediary in disputes between the Suriname natives and the English colonists.

Oroonoko can only be appeased and distracted from thoughts of returning home for so long, and he begins to talk to the other slaves about escaping. They are loyal to him and follow him into the jungle. The deputy governor of the English colony in Suriname, named Byam, is brought in to help pursue Oroonoko and the slaves he has incited to escape. When they are surrounded by the English, the slaves initially fight by Oroonoko's side, but they are convinced by Byam to return with him to the plantation and to abandon Oroonoko. Forced to surrender, Oroonoko is brutally beaten.

As he begins to heal from his assault, Oroonoko realizes that he will probably still be executed, and if he is gone, Imoinda will be in grave danger. Both Oroonoko and Imoinda agree that she will suffer punishments worse than death at the hands of the English. The two escape into the jungle, and with Imoinda's blessing, Oroonoko kills the pregnant Imoinda. For two days he grieves by her body. When he realizes that he must go, as he has vowed to revenge himself and Imoinda on those who have captured them, Oroonoko finds that he is too weak to move. He languishes for another six days by Imoinda's body.

Another slave, named Tuscan, leads a search party to find Oroonoko and Imoinda. When Tuscan and another man from this party come upon Oroonoko, Oroonoko realizes he will not be able to carry out his revenge. Instead, he seeks to kill himself, and begins attacking his own body with his knife. Tuscan and the others are finally able to overcome him, and they return him to the plantation. There, he is operated on, his wounds closed, and he is revived, only so that his captors can execute him in their own manner. He is dismembered and finally killed.

Aboan

Aboan is a fellow soldier in the army of the Coramantien community. He fights alongside Oroonoko, under Oroonoko's leadership. Aboan is romantically involved with Onahal, the former mistress of the old king. Oroonoko establishes a chain of communication to Imoinda by passing messages to Aboan, who relates Oroonoko's feelings to Onahal, who finally delivers the messages to Imoinda.

Byam

Byam is the deputy governor of the English colony in Suriname. He is known for his brutal nature, according to Behn. It is Byam who leads the search for Oroonoko and the escaped slaves, and he who convinces the other slaves to abandon Oroonoko. At Byam's orders, Oroonoko is beaten and tortured, and later, after Oroonoko's murder of Imoinda and subsequent recapture, it is Byam who insists that Oroonoko, who has been almost fatally injured by his own hand, is healed and restored to health before he is tortured, dismembered, and executed. In Byam, Behn depicts the cruelest elements of the slave holding system. All the evils of slavery rest almost exclusively on his shoulders, as the other whites Oroonoko encounters, save the

English captain who tricks him, all treat him with a great deal of respect.

Caesar

See Oroonoko

Clemene

See Imoinda

Imoinda

Imoinda is the fifteen-year-old daughter of a fallen general, who was a man Oroonoko revered as a father. When Oroonoko presents Imoinda with slaves captured in battle as a means of honoring her and her dead father, Oroonoko is stunned by Imoinda's beauty. She becomes the object of Oroonoko's fierce passion and love. Imoinda soon confides to Oroonoko that she shares his feelings. Although Imoinda feels bound by duty and tradition —and fear of death—to accept the king's royal veil (his demand that she become his mistress), she, nevertheless, remains emotionally faithful to Oroonoko. When she allows him to visit her in her chambers and spends a romantic night with him, she is punished for disgracing the king; she is sold into slavery.

When the reader once again encounters Imoinda on the plantation to which she has been sold, she is again defined only by her beauty. Just as

Oroonoko became entranced with her due to her beauty, and the king sought to possesses her because of her beauty, so do all the other slaves on the plantation desire her, according to the overseer, Trefry. Imoinda's beauty makes her an object of desire, and she is loyal to Oroonoko, gladly welcoming the fate he has decided for her—to be murdered at his hand rather than risk being tortured by the deputy governor Byam. Yet, Behn reveals little else about Imoinda beyond her physical characteristics. A sense of duty commingled with fear are the driving forces behind her actions.

The King

The king, usually referred to as "the old king," is the leader of Oroonoko's people in Coramantien, and he is the grandfather of Oroonoko. Behn describes him as over one hundred years old. He has numerous wives and mistresses. His desire is rekindled by Imoinda, and he orders her to become his mistress even though she is already committed to Oroonoko. He cares not whether Imoinda feels any affection for him, knowing that she will see it as her duty to submit to him, which she does. Nevertheless, he jealously watches any interaction Imoinda has with Oroonoko, going into a rage, for example, when Imoinda accidentally trips and falls into Oroonoko's arms during a dance she is commanded to perform for the king and his generals. When the king discovers that Oroonoko has stolen into Imoinda's chambers and has been with her, he sells Imoinda into slavery out of spite and jealously, knowing it would be more honorable to have her killed. He lies, letting it be known to Oroonoko that Imoinda has been executed. The king seeks Oroonoko's forgiveness and realizes he has wronged him, but he does so out of fear of Oroonoko's rebellion rather than out of genuine remorse.

Narrator

In the dedicatory letter and in the opening paragraphs of the novel, Behn identifies herself as the narrator of the story. She remains a significant presence throughout the novel, commenting on events from her own perspective and describing her own interaction with the other characters. While Behn asserts that the story is true and although she appears in the novel as an eyewitness, it is believed that the work is a fictionalized account of Behn's experiences. As many facts about her life are unknown, critics have been unable to verify enough of the details she gives in the novel to label it as nonfiction, despite Behn's assertions to the contrary. Yet it has been observed that many of her descriptions of Suriname in the mid-seventeenth century are accurate enough to contend that Behn likely visited the English colony at some time.

Onahal

Onahal is an older woman, who is described as still beautiful. She was once one of the king's many mistresses. Like other mistresses of whom the king has tired, Onahal now tends to the newer, younger mistresses, and she is assigned to Imoinda after Imoinda arrives. Onahal and Aboan are romantically involved, and through this couple, Imoinda and Oroonoko communicate. Onahal helps arrange the fateful night that Oroonoko and Imoinda share, the event that results in Imoinda being sold into slavery.

Oroonoko

Oroonoko is a seventeen-year-old prince in the community of African people living in Coramantien. He becomes a general when his own general dies. Behn describes the nobility of Oroonoko in glowing terms. His physical perfection is admired as much as the integrity of his soul. In Behn's accounting of Oroonoko's physical traits, he is distinguished from other Africans and described in terms of his resemblance to Europeans. His love for Imoinda is also depicted in such a way as to highlight Oroonoko's purity of affection. Behn comments that in love, Oroonoko is even more honorable than Christians. His desire for Imoinda is described in physical terms; he longs to be with her, and he risks both of their lives in order to spend the night with her. After Imoinda has been sold into slavery, Oroonoko, who has been told that Imoinda has been executed, accepts the king's apologies and vows to never raise a weapon against him in revenge. Oroonoko languishes in his tent, despite the fact that his fellow soldiers beg him to lead them in battle. He finally collects himself and fights as though he seeks death. Oroonoko's anguish is intended by Behn to be regarded as a mark of his love for Imoinda and to indicate the depths of his grief for her.

Once Oroonoko himself has been sold as a slave in Suriname, having been tricked by the English captain, his nobility, according to Behn, is apparent to all. Although he is still bought as a slave, he is set apart from the other slaves and allowed freedoms the others do not possess. Promises are made that he will be allowed to return home, but they are never fulfilled. Oroonoko's reunion with Imoinda on the plantation is viewed with wonder by the white people on the plantation. Oroonoko and Imoinda are treated as curiosities, and they are allowed to live together. While Behn notes that she spends time visiting with Oroonoko and Imoinda, in general the whites' attitude toward the couple is one of amazement that slaves could demonstrate personal nobility, beauty, and affection for one another.

After Imoinda becomes pregnant, Oroonoko's captors begin to fear that he will rebel against them, as he is persistent in his attempts to bargain for his and Imoinda's freedom. He is given various tasks and duties in order to distract him from his goal and to make him feel purposeful. Behn demonstrates, through her recounting of Oroonoko's fate after he attempts to lead the slaves in escaping from the plantation, that it is Oroonoko's difference from the other slaves that results in his torture and ultimate death. He is clearly a leader and obviously a man who is certain that he, unlike his fellow slaves, does not deserve to be made subservient to others. Although he attempts to help free the other slaves, initially he only bargains for his own and Imoinda's freedom. It is also Oroonoko himself who, while still in Africa, sold many of the slaves to the English in the first place. Behn demonstrates Oroonoko's praiseworthy qualities—his ability to love Imoinda, his leadership qualities, his sense of honor. At the same time, these qualities lead to Oroonoko's death. His love for Imoinda leads him to murder her, to protect her from a fate worse than death. His abilities as a leader result in his punishment for tempting the slaves to escape. His sense of honor leads him to seek revenge against those who would hold him against his will, and this desire to violently attack Byam and his men, although he is unsuccessful in his efforts, results in Oroonoko's torture and execution.

Trefry

Trefry is the overseer of the slaves at the plantation where Oroonoko is destined. Trefry purchases Oroonoko but is so impressed with his nobility and intelligence that he does not treat him as a slave, and he even promises to obtain Oroonoko's freedom. While it is unlikely that Trefry ever intended to keep this promise, he does treat Oroonoko with respect, and he serves as an advocate for Oroonoko throughout much of Oroonoko's time at the plantation. After Oroonoko leads the slaves in an escape attempt, it is Trefry who prevents Oroonoko from being hanged on Byam's orders. In the end, Trefry is unable to protect Oroonoko.

Tuscan

Tuscan is another slave on the plantation to which Oroonoko has been sold. When Oroonoko tries to convince the slaves to follow him and escape their life of slavery, Tuscan confirms the slaves' loyalty to Oroonoko but also questions Oroonoko. Specifically, Tuscan points to the fact that the slaves all have families, and they do not wish to jeopardize the lives of their wives and children. Oroonoko still manages to convince Tuscan and the others. Tuscan stands beside Oroonoko and refuses to yield when the escaped slaves are captured by Byam. He is whipped alongside Oroonoko. When Oroonoko and Imoinda escape together so that Oroonoko can kill her, Tuscan is with the search party sent out to look for them. He attempts to help Oroonoko, but he is injured by Oroonoko in the process.

Slavery

Behn's treatment of the issue of slavery in the seventeenth century is consistent with the commonly held opinions of the English population of that time period. Throughout *Oroonoko*, Behn depicts slavery as a practical economic necessity; there is little indication that she objected to slavery as an institution. However, Behn presents Oroonoko as an uncommonly noble African, and as such, a man who should not be a slave. In describing Oroonoko's own role in the slave trade with the English, Behn emphasizes her view of Oroonoko's superiority over his fellow Africans. This superiority, according to Behn, is acknowledged by the slaves Oroonoko has sold. When he encounters them on the plantation in Suriname, Oroonoko is still received as a prince by his former countrymen. He is honored and respected rather than attacked for his role in their current imprisonment.

In discussing the native people of Suriname, Behn describes them as innocent children. Her tone, which is condescending in the way she depicts their native habits, reflects the attitude of an imperialist nation. At the same time, the innocent and peaceful nature of the native people is not what keeps them from being enslaved by the English colonists, as Behn points out. Rather, the English are outnumbered by the native population, and they are also dependent on them for their knowledge of the land. While Behn illustrates the cruelty of the actions against Oroonoko taken by the deputy governor of the English colony in Suriname (Byam), she does not do so as a means of protesting the slave holding system. Other whites, herself and Trefry included, treat Oroonoko with respect, and few other transgressions against the slaves—save their being held as slaves—are described. Slavery, then in *Oroonoko*, may be viewed as a backdrop to the story of the tragic hero Oroonoko and his love Imoinda, providing the dramatic conflict required in such romantic tales.

Love

The love between Oroonoko and Imoinda in *Oroonoko* is lauded by Behn for its passion as well as its purity. Oroonoko and Imoinda desire only each other, despite the fact that Imoinda is forced to serve as the king's mistress. They epitomize tragic lovers not only in their devotion to one another and their nobility of spirit, but also in that they are forced apart. Even though the king knows that Oroonoko and Imoinda are romantically involved, he nonetheless indulges his desire for the beautiful young girl and demands that she become his mistress. Oroonoko cannot act to save her as her life, and his, would be in jeopardy. Imoinda also knows that death awaits those girls who refuse to accept the king's royal veil, the token of his desire for them. Still the pair risks their lives to be together.

Once they are reunited as slaves on the plantation, their love is admired and honored by their white captors; they are allowed to live together. The honorable Oroonoko, however, seeks to return to his homeland with his pregnant wife rather than remain at the plantation, even though he lives a unique life for a slave (he is not required to labor). After leading the slaves in an unsuccessful escape, Oroonoko is punished, and he knows that if he is executed, Imoinda will suffer at the hands of the cruel deputy governor, Byam, and that his unborn child will enter into the world as a slave. The lovers embrace the only fate that seems acceptable; the only escape from slavery and torture is death. Imoinda welcomes death at her lover's hand, and after she is gone, Oroonoko mourns her for so long he is unable to seek revenge on his captors. While he then attempts to kill himself, he is prevented from doing so, only to be tortured and executed.

In *Oroonoko*, Behn explores the details attendant to the notion of tragic love—her noble lovers are forced apart and meet a terrible fate. At the same time, Behn, who authored numerous erotic poems, incorporates into her story erotic elements of physical love. She makes it clear that one of the components of the attraction between Oroonoko and Imoinda is a powerful physical desire for one another, a desire that Oroonoko and Imoinda indulge to their detriment.

Topics for Further Study

- *Oroonoko* has been compared to Harriet Beecher Stowe's *Uncle Tom's Cabin*, published in 1852, in that both authors depict brutalities endured by slaves in a plantation society. To explore this issue further, take one of two approaches. Either read Stowe's novel and compare Stowe's treatment of slavery to Behn's, or research the scholarly criticism on Stowe's treatment of slavery; use these critical responses as a means of comparing Stowe's attitudes with Behn's. In your opinion, can both works legitimately be called emancipation novels? How do the authors explore racial issues? Prepare a persuasive essay in which you present your view on whether Behn's novel is justifiably compared to Stowe's as an abolitionist novel.

- In the opening pages of *Oroonoko*, Behn offers a description of the land and people of seventeenth-century Suriname. Research the people and culture of modern Suriname. How does the nation's modern culture reflect its Dutch and English colonial history? What are the nation's culinary, literary, and musical traditions? Create a presentation for your class. Incorporate visual elements, such as copies of photographs of the people, landscape, and food of Suriname, for example. You may wish to instead create a Web page that incorporates these images, along with a sampling of local music or video clips related to the people or traditions of the nation.

- In 1739, playwright Thomas Southerne produced a drama based on Behn's *Oroonoko*. Read Southerne's adaptation of Behn's novel (available online through Google Books). How does Southerne's version of the material treat Behn's text? Does the playwright make drastic changes?Do his revisions alter Behn's themes? Are the characters as Southerne treats them substantially different from Behn's characterizations? Write a comparative essay in which you explore these topics.

- In *Oroonoko*, Behn explores the English colonization of Suriname in the mid-to late seventeenth century. England had other colonies throughout the world at this time as well. Research English colonization during the mid-to late-seventeenth century. Where were the other English colonies located? Did the English use slave labor in other colonies, as it did in Suriname on the sugar plantations? What were the relationships like between the English and the native people of the colonies? Prepare a written report, a PowerPoint presentation, or a Web page in which you share your findings. Be sure to cite all of your sources.

- Behn explores the fate of Oroonoko after he has been sold into slavery, discussing his life in Africa, tracing his journey to Suriname, and following his experiences there. In the young-adult novel *The Glory Field* (1994), written by Walter

Dean Myers, the author similarly follows the experiences of a young man, Muhammed Bilal, who is captured in Sierra Leone in Africa and sold as a slave in the American colonies in 1753. While Myers's work is set in a later time period than Behn's, the two novels feature young African men sold to British colonies in the Americas (Muhammed in North America, Oroonoko in South America). With a book group, read Myers's novel and compare it with Behn's. In what ways do Muhammed's and Oroonoko's experiences seem similar? How are the English portrayed in both works? Do the characters share a similar fate? How do the authors' different perspectives impact the tone they use in their novels? With your group, present your comparison to the class as an oral report.

Style

First-Person Narration

Behn composes her novel *Oroonoko* in the first person. She incorporates a narrator who observes the events of the story and refers to herself as "I." In this type of story, the narrator is often associated with the author, although this assumption is sometimes erroneous, as the author of the story may be creating a narrator whose opinions and observations are meant to be taken ironically or as a satire of the prevailing opinions of the author's society. (Satire is the use of humor, irony, or exaggeration, for example, in order to expose faults or shortcomings.) Behn, however, in her dedication to *Oroonoko*, makes it clear that she is the narrator of the work, which she claims to be a true story. Modern critics generally regard the work as a fictionalized account by Behn, and the narrator she depicts in the work as a fictionalized version of herself. Whether or not Behn's narrator is regarded as Behn herself or a fictionalized version of herself, the work is still regarded as a reflection of Behn's own views on such themes as slavery and her notion of love.

A Hybrid Genre: Tragic Romance and Travel Literature

Many critics have observed that in *Oroonoko*, Behn combines two popular genres, that of the tragic romance and the travelogue. Laura Anne Doyle, in the 2008 *Freedom's Empire: Race and the Rise of the Novel in Atlantic Modernity, 1640–1940*, states that Behn combines stories of "exotic adventure in Suriname" with "the high, tragic romance of noble lovers from Africa," along with "the brutal depiction of a colonial slave revolt." Similarly, Janet Todd in the 1998 *The Critical Fortunes of Aphra Behn*, observes that Behn "presents an old-fashioned romantic tale in the modern guise of a true travelogue, which allows her to assume authority." Behn, a successful dramatist, drew on the dramatic tradition available to her, incorporating elements of tragic romance plays into a story based on her travels to Suriname. Predecessors, including William Shakespeare (whom Behn was known to admire), and contemporary dramatists, including John Dryden, made frequent use of the tragic romance genre as well. In the tragic romance, lovers are prevented by circumstances from being together. The tragic hero is a brave and noble man with a fatal flaw that leads to his downfall, and the tragic heroine, like the hero, typically dies for the sake of love. Seventeenth century travelogues often focused on the colonization of the New World. Like Captain John Smith's 1624 *Generall Historie of Virginia* and his 1630 *True Travels*, New World travelogues were nonfiction accounts of travelers or colonists to the Americas, and they often explored the relationship between Europeans and the native inhabitants of these lands. Behn's work combines these elements, an allegedly truthful account of her time in Suriname and the tragic romance, complete with tragic lovers, who, like their Shakespearean predecessors Romeo and Juliet, would rather die than live without the other.

Seventeenth-Century English Colonialism in Suriname

In the seventeenth century, the north coastal region of South America was the object of English, Dutch, and French colonial desires, as the region had not yet been settled by European colonists. The English Lord Willoughby, who had founded a colony in Barbados, an island in the Caribbean Sea, sent a party in 1650 to the Suriname region. Plantations were successfully established. Willoughby appointed William Byam as the colony's deputy governor. By the 1660s, the colony's plantations were producing sugar for the English market and incorporating slave labor in order to do so. From 1665 through 1667, the Second Anglo-Dutch War was fought, when the Dutch attempted to wrest from the English the land they colonized in Suriname. Suriname was ceded to the Dutch, while the English claimed New Amsterdam in Guyana. The Third Anglo-Dutch War was fought from 1672 to 1674. The Dutch reconquered New Amsterdam, while the English reclaimed Suriname. These possessions were reversed, however, by the Treaty of Westminster, signed in 1674 by King Charles II of England. Scholars do not know for certain when Behn visited Suriname, but by the time her book was published in 1688, Suriname had been lost to the Dutch.

Seventeenth-Century Slave Trade in Africa

The English colonies in the Caribbean, including Willoughby's Barbados and Suriname colonies, were in need of laborers to be used in sugar production. Although some indentured laborers were sent from Ireland, Scotland, and Wales, the plantations needed more workers than could be serviced in this fashion. (Indentured servants worked in conditions similar to those endured by slaves, but were under contract to work for a specified amount of time, usually several years.) King Charles I, in 1630, granted the English slave-trafficking rights, and by 1672 the English had established the Royal African Company for the purposes of developing the slave trade in Africa. The Dutch competed with the English for the acquisition of slaves from Africa. As Janet Todd explains in her introduction to the 2003 edition of *Oroonoko*, the trade in African slaves in which the English and Dutch participated was "carried on by permission of the slave-selling African chiefs." Todd further observes that in the seventeenth century, the English did not enslave Africans exclusively, nor did they do so for racial reasons. Todd explains that the English in Barbados had white slaves, used European indentured servants as slaves, and on board ships and in English colonial settlements, Catholics and Protestants at various times enslaved the other group. Other scholars demonstrate the rapidity with which the slave trade developed to service the sugar industry in the English Caribbean settlements. In their introduction to the 2000 edition of Behn's novel, Catherine Gallagher and Simon Stern state: "Slavery became the dominant institution of the English Caribbean in less than a generation.... A few decades transformed the region into a ruthlessly efficient machine for supplying Europe with cheap sugar." At some point during this process, the critics suggest, slavery did become racialized. The Royal African Company was active in slave trading until the 1730s, at which point the British accomplished the task through other means. British slave trading was not abolished until 1807.

Compare & Contrast

- **1660s:** The English governor of the newly established colony of Suriname, Lord Willoughby, attempts to build the area of the West Indies, including Suriname and Barbados, into a sugar producing empire. He turns to acquiring slave labor from Africa to meet this goal.

  1680s: Suriname is lost to the Dutch in the Second Anglo-Dutch War, recaptured by the English in the Third Anglo-Dutch War, and eventually restored to the Dutch by the 1674 Treaty of Westminster.

Today: Suriname is officially known as the Republic of Suriname, having won independence from the Netherlands in 1975. The lasting colonial influence of the English and the Dutch is revealed in that the nation's official language is Dutch, while English is also commonly spoken.

- **1660s:** King Charles II rules England. While the political parties of the Tories and Whigs battle over the balance of power in the English government (the Tories are advocates for the centralization of power with the monarch, while the Whigs maintain that Parliament should have more power), the bubonic plague sweeps over England in 1665, and in 1666, more devastation occurs with the Great Fire of London.

1680s: King James II ascends the throne in 1685 after the death of his brother, Charles II. As a Roman Catholic, James is the target of heated criticism from his Protestant opposition. Largely due to the political conflicts aroused by these religious differences, James abdicates the throne in 1689. In his absence, King William and Queen Mary are crowned as the new monarchs of England.

Today: The reigning monarch of the United Kingdom is Queen Elizabeth II. In 1707, with the signing of the Act of Union by Queen Anne, England and Scotland united to form the Kingdom of Great Britain. The United Kingdom, as of 1801, now also includes Northern Ireland. The role of the monarch of the United Kingdom of Great Britain and Northern Ireland is ceremonial, and the governance of the United Kingdom is handled by the prime minister and Parliament. Gordon Brown is prime minister in the second decade of the twenty-first century.

- **1660s:** There are few female writers in England at this time, and those that are known are largely prominent only within a small circle of admirers. Margaret Cavendish receives greater attention than most female writers for her poetry, the first volume of which was *Poems and Fancies* and was published in 1653, as well as for her plays and miscellaneous works on philosophy.

  1680s: The number of female

writers in England remains relatively small. Some, like Behn, however, achieve prominence. Behn is a prolific writer of plays and becomes as well known as her male counterpart, John Dryden. Behn also becomes England's first female novelist with the publication of *Oroonoko* in 1688.

Today: There is no shortage of female novelists in the United Kingdom. Authors of popular fiction, including J. K. Rowling, as well as authors of literary fiction, including Bernardine Evaristo, Gaynor Arnold, and Lissa Evans, abound. In 2009, Evaristo, Arnold, and Evans are all long-listed for the prestigious literary fiction award, the Orange Prize.

England in the Mid-to Late Seventeenth Century

The mid-seventeenth century was a time of great religious conflict, royal power struggles, and natural disaster in England. When Behn was a young girl, in 1649, King Charles I was executed in the aftermath of the Civil War, in which supporters of Charles battled the supporters of Parliament. The war was largely concerned with the balance of power between the king and the members of Parliament. The Puritan military leader Oliver Cromwell became the head of state and later, in 1653, was named Lord Protector. He refused the offer of the throne, and after his death in 1658, he was succeeded as Lord Protector by his son. Richard Cromwell, however, was unsuccessful in maintaining the Protectorate status of England, and in 1660, Charles II, who had been exiled to France, returned to England and claimed the throne.

Tensions regarding political power continued to divide the English government. The Tory Royalists served as advocates for the restoration of the powers of the king, while Whigs insisted on the use of Parliament as a means of balancing, or limiting, royal powers. During Charles II's reign, the bubonic plague devoured England in 1665, and this calamity was followed in 1666 by the Great Fire of London, which destroyed much of the city. The religious conflicts between Roman Catholics, the Church of England (also known as the Anglican Church, a Protestant church that incorporated some elements of Catholicism), and nonconforming Protestants (those Protestants, also known as Puritans, who fought for an English Protestant Church completely free from Catholic influence), continued to create political controversy. In 1662, the Act of Uniformity was passed, requiring the use of a common prayer book and demanding that clergy members conform to Anglican doctrines. In 1673, nonconforming Protestants and Roman Catholics were excluded from holding civil and military offices by the passage of the Test Act.

Charles II died in 1685 and was succeeded by his brother James II. James was a Roman Catholic, and, not surprisingly, conflicts with Protestants ensued. James abdicated the throne in 1689 and the Protestant King William and Queen Mary were crowned.

Critical Overview

Published in 1688, shortly before Behn's death a year later, *Oroonoko* received the attention commensurate with the work of a popular author, and the work is commonly regarded as the most successful of her novels. As Frederick M. Link observes in the 1968 *Aphra Behn*, the novel additionally "had a topical interest derived from its setting in a colony recently lost to the Dutch." (The English colony in Suriname was attacked by the Dutch in 1667, and ceded to them by treaty in 1674.) Part of the lasting appeal of the work was due to its dramatization by playwright Thomas Southerne in the early eighteenth century, according to Janet Todd in the 1998 *The Critical Fortunes of Aphra Behn*. Abolitionist attitudes during the eighteenth century additionally contributed to the novel's continued popularity, Todd explains. By the early twentieth century, the abolitionist label was still being applied to Behn's novel due to her sympathies toward Oroonoko, and her depiction of the cruelties he endures. In a 1913 introduction to *The Novels of Mrs. Aphra Behn*, Ernest A. Baker regards *Oroonoko* as "the first emancipation novel," and compares Behn's dedication to the cause to "the same feeling of outraged humanity that in after days inflamed Mrs. Stowe" (the author of the antislavery novel *Uncle Tom's Cabin*, published in 1852). While Montague Summers, in the introduction to the reprint of *Oroonoko* in the 1916 *Oroonoko &*

Other Prose Narratives by Aphra Behn, questions Baker's assertion, Summers does agree that Behn conveyed genuine "sympathy with the oppressed blacks." Summers goes on to examine the work's literary elements and to praise the lyric quality of Behn's prose as well as her ability to capture the details of her setting. Baker explores Behn's theme of man's savagery toward man, arguing that Behn paints Oroonoko as the "ideal man" and that she contrasts his noble actions with the "vicious manners of the colonists."

Later critics have focused on the work's structure and style, studying the way Behn combined elements of the tragic romance with the conventions of the novel and of the travelogue. As Lore Metzger asserts in the 1973 introduction to *Oroonoko, or the Royal Slave*, "Behn's fusion of romance motifs with novelistic verisimilitude does not consistently produce both wonder and delight." However, Metzger goes on, the attempt is an interesting one in the way it plays to the exploration of the "favorite Renaissance themes," such as the "antithesis of innocent natural and corrupt civilized man." Frederick Link similarly comments on this contrast in his literary biography *Aphra Behn*, but he points out that Behn takes pains to associate Oroonoko with European tradition. He is "not a true savage, nor is his nobility inherent." Rather, Link observes, the "true primitives in the story are the native Indians." Like Metzger, Catherine Gallagher and Simon Stern, in their introduction to the 2000 edition of Behn's *Oroonoko; or, The Royal Slave*, study Behn's attempt to employ different genres or styles in her work. Gallagher and Stern maintain that Behn did not seek to serve as a chronicler of slavery in the region of Suriname, but instead "to blend three popular forms of Restoration literature: the New World travel story, the courtly romance, and the heroic tragedy." Unlike their critical counterparts in the early twentieth century, Gallagher and Stern find no traces of an emancipatory spirit in Behn's writing. They argue that Behn portrays slavery "as a practical economic matter; it neither needs nor gets transcendental authorization." Finally, Gallagher and Stern comment on the parallels between Behn as author/narrator and Oroonoko. The critics contend that Behn likens herself to Oroonoko by pointing out that they are both recognized as superior to the locals in Suriname, that "like him, she appears a shining marvel when she travels to the Indian village; and like his words, hers are always supposed to be truthful."

What Do I Read Next?

- Behn achieved acclaim as a playwright before her novel *Oroonoko* was published in 1688. The Oxford World Classics edition of Behn's dramatic works *The Rover and Other Plays*, published in 2008, contains Behn's best-known play, *The Rover*, which was originally published in 1677, along with several of Behn's comedies and satires.

- In Angeline Goreau's *Reconstructing Aphra: A Social Biography of Aphra Behn*, published in 1980 by Dial Press, Goreau attempts to place what little is known about Behn's life into social, historical, and cultural contexts.

- John Dryden was Behn's contemporary and a fellow playwright. His drama *All for Love*, originally published in 1677, is counted among Dryden's most acclaimed. The work is a romantic tragedy concerned with the historical lovers Antony and Cleopatra. *All for Love* is available through Echo Library, and was published in 2007.

- *Caribbean Exchanges: Slavery and*

the Transformation of English Society, 1640–1700 by Susan Dwyer Amussen, published by the University of North Carolina Press in 2007, explores the history of the English colonies in the Caribbean in the mid-to late seventeenth century. Amussen studies the colonists' use of slaves in the production of sugar and additionally explores the ways in which colonial experiences shaped cultural and national identity in England.

- Editor Paula Burnett offers a collection of poetry by Caribbean writers in *The Penguin Book of Caribbean Verse in English*, published by Penguin Global in 2006. Burnett's collection features works from the Caribbean oral tradition, including centuries-old slave songs, as well as poetry from contemporary Caribbean poets.

- *Sold for Silver: An Autobiography of a Girl Sold into Slavery in Southeast Asia*, by Janet Lim, like *Oroonoko*, is the story of an individual who is forced into a life of slavery. Lim's work, however, is an autobiographical account by a Chinese woman of her life as a slave in Singapore in the 1930s and beyond. The work was originally published in 1958 and is available in a 2005 edition published by Monsoon Books.

- Sharon M. Draper's *Copper Sun*, published in 2006 by Athenaeum Books for Young Readers, is a young-adult novel that traces the experiences of a fifteen-year-old African girl who is sold into slavery in eighteenth century America. While Draper's work is intended for teen audiences, it does, like *Oroonoko*, contain some graphic details concerning the brutalities suffered by slaves.

- Editors Elspeth Graham, Hilary Hinds, Elaine Hobby, and Helen Wilcox collect autobiographical essays by seventeenth-century English poets and essayists in *Her Own Life: Autobiographical Writings by Seventeenth Century Englishwomen*, published by Routledge in 1989. The collection offers a glimpse into the daily life of women during this time period.

Sources

"Act of Union, 1707," in *United Kingdom Parliament*, http://www.parliament.uk/actofunion/index.html (accessed January 2, 2010).

Baker, Ernest A., Introduction to *The Novels of Mrs. Aphra Behn*, by Aphra Behn, George Routledge & Sons, 1913, pp. vii—xxvii.

Behn, Aphra, *Oroonoko*, Penguin Books, 2003.

"Charles I," "Interregnum," "Charles II," "James II," and "William III and Mary II," in *The Official Web site of the British Monarchy*, http://www.royal.gov.uk/HistoryoftheMonarchy/His (accessed December 27, 2009).

Cooley, Ron, et al., "Margaret (Lucas) Cavendish, Duchess of Newcastle (1623–1673)," in *Luminarium: Anthology of English Literature*, http://www.luminarium.org/sevenlit/cavendish/caveı (accessed January 2, 2010).

Doyle, Laura Anne, "Entering Atlantic History: Oroonoko, Imoinda, and Behn," in *Freedom's Empire: Race and the Rise of the Novel in Atlantic Modernity, 1640–1940*, Duke University Press, 2008, pp. 97–117.

Gallagher, Catherine, and Simon Stern, eds., "Introduction: Cultural and Historical Background," in *Oroonoko; or, The Royal Slave*, by Aphra Behn, Bedford/St. Martin's, 2000, pp. 3–25.

Hoefte, Rosemarijn, "A Concise History of Suriname and Marienburg," in *In Place of Slavery: A Social History of British Indian and Javanese Laborers in Suriname*, University Press of Florida, 1998, pp. 8–24.

Hooker, Richard, "The European Enlightenment: The Case of England," in *Washington State University's World Civilizations Internet Classroom and Anthology*, http://www.wsu.edu/~dee/ENLIGHT/ENGLAND.HTM (accessed January 2, 2010).

Link, Frederick M., "The Novelist," in *Aphra Behn*, Twayne Publishers, 1968, pp. 130–51.

Metzger, Lore, Introduction to *Oroonoko, or the Royal Slave*, by Aphra Behn, W. W. Norton, 1973, pp. ix—xv.

"Orange Prize for Fiction 2009 Longlist," in *Orange Prize for Fiction*, http://www.orangeprize.co.uk/show/feature/orangep 2009-longlist (accessed January 2, 2010).

Porter, Andrew, "Britain's Empire in 1815," in *BBC's British History In-Depth*, http://www.bbc.co.uk/history/british/empire_seapow (accessed January 2, 2010).

Summers, Montague, ed., Introduction to *Oroonoko; or, The Royal Slave*, in*Oroonoko & Other Prose Narratives by Aphra Behn*, Benjamin Blom, 1916, reprint, 1967, pp. 127–29.

"Suriname," in *CIA: World Factbook*, https://www.cia.gov/library/publications/the-world-factbook/geos/ns.html (accessed January 2, 2010).

Todd, Janet, Introduction to *Oroonoko*, by Aphra Behn, Penguin Books, 2003, pp. xv—xxxv.

Todd, Janet, Notes to *Oroonoko*, by Aphra Behn, Penguin Books, 2003, pp. 79–99.

Todd, Janet, "*Oroonoko*," in *The Critical Fortunes of Aphra Behn*, Camden House, 1998, pp. 114–30.

Walvin, James, "Ending It All: The Crusade Against Slavery," in *Black Ivory: Slavery in the British Empire*, 2nd ed., Blackwell, 2001, pp. 259–71.

Further Reading

Azim, Firdous, *The Colonial Rise of the Novel: From Aphra Behn to Charlotte Bronte*, Routledge, 1993.

> From a feminist perspective, Azim explores the work of female novelists writing during the years of English colonial expansion, examining the impact of England's imperialism on the writings of Behn and Bronte. In particular, Azim studies issues of gender and identity in the works of these women.

Morgan, Kenneth, *Slavery and the British Empire: From Africa to America*, Oxford University Press, 2007.

> Morgan investigates the history of the British slave trade, studying the ways in which the British used slavery as a means of expanding their colonial empire.

Morris, Mervyn, *Making West Indian Literature*, Ian Randle Publishers, 2004.

> Morris examines the development of modern West Indian literature and comments on the way the colonial history of the West Indies shaped the area's notions of identity, and

subsequently influenced the literature of the region.

Scott, John A., *Settlers on the Eastern Shore: The British Colonies in North America, 1607–1750*, Facts on File, 1991.

> Scott discusses the British colonization of North America in the seventeenth and eighteenth centuries. The work, which is targeted at a young adult audience, employs such primary sources as letters and diaries in order to covey what daily life was like for British settlers in American colonies. Scott additionally details the relationships between the colonists and the Native American people they encountered and discusses the colonists' use of slaves and indentured servants.

Todd, Janet, *The Secret Life of Aphra Behn*, Rutgers University Press, 1997.

> Todd, who has edited Behn's writings, provides an examination of what is known about Behn's life and incorporates this scant biographical information with a detailed critical analysis of Behn's body of work.

Suggested Search Terms

Oroonoko AND Behn

Aphra Behn

Behn AND slavery

Behn AND seventeenth-century novel

Oroonoko AND colonialism

Oroonoko AND tragic romance

Oroonoko AND travelogue

Oroonoko analysis

Oroonoko AND abolitionism

Oroonoko AND royalism

Oroonoko AND racism

9 781375 385916